anythink

# Find Your Future in Art

**Kim Childress**

Created and produced by
Bright Futures Press, Cary, North Carolina
www.brightfuturespress.com

Published by
Cherry Lake Publishing, Ann Arbor, Michigan
www.cherrylakepublishing.com

Photo Credits: cover, Shutterstock/kozirksy; cover, Shutterstock/alphaspirit; cover, Shutterstock/gui jun peng; cover, Shutterstock/scyther5; page 4 (top), Shutterstock/kosmos111; page 4 (left), Shutterstock/Postive Vectors; page 6 (top), Shutterstock/alphaspirit; page 6 (left), Shutterstock/WAJ; page 7, Shutterstock/Grimgram; page 8, Gene J Puskar/AP; page 9 (top), Shutterstock/Christos Georghiou; page 9 (left), Shutterstock/Reginast777; page 10, Shutterstock/Igor Zakowski; page 11, Shutterstock/Nearbirds; page 12 (top), Shutterstock/scyther5; page 12 (left), Shutterstock/ekler; page 13, Shutterstock/Fotinia; page 14, Shutterstock/Naphat_Jorgee; page 15 (top), Shutterstock/Kozirksy; page 15 (left), Shutterstock/alexwhite; page 16, Shutterstock/yitewang; page 17, Shutterstock/Brian A Jackson; page 18 (top), Shutterstock/Kikujungboy; page 18 (left), Shutterstock/MastekA; page 19, Shutterstock/Lorelyn Medina; page 20, Shutterstock/QQ7; page 21 (top), Shutterstock/Diego Cervo; page 21 (left) Shutterstock/Lightspring; page 22, Shutterstock/sibgat; page 23, Shutterstock/Alexander Tokstykh; page 24 (top), Shutterstock/gui jun peng; page 24 (left), Shutterstock/Andrey Burmakin; page 25, Shutterstock/Macrovector; page 26, Shutterstock/aaron choi; page 27 (top), Shutterstock/Leszek Glasner; page 27, (left) Shutterstock/Valery Brozhinsky; page 28, Shutterstock/Mayrum; page 29, Shutterstock/Syda Productions.

Editorial Contributor: Kelly White

Library of Congress Cataloging-in-Publication Date

Names: Childress, Kim, author.
Title: Find your future in art / By Kim Childress.
Description: Ann Arbor, Michigan : Cherry Lake Publishing, 2016. | Includes index.
Identifiers: LCCN 2016008204| ISBN 9781634719018 (hardcover) | ISBN 9781634719247 (pdf) | ISBN 9781634719476 (pbk.) | ISBN 9781634719704 (ebook)
Subjects:  LCSH: Arts--Vocational guidance--Juvenile literature.
Classification: LCC NX163 .C49 2016 | DDC 700.23--dc23
LC record available at http://lccn.loc.gov/2016008204

Printed in the United States of America.

# Table of Contents

**Find Your Future in Art**

# Find your future in art

When you think of art, what comes to mind? Paintings? Sculptures? Advertisements? Museums? All are correct! The world of art is all around you!

That last LEGO® kit you put together? It takes an artist who is also an engineer to design those awesome products as well as brainstorm the next great creation. Cars, clothes, logos, signs, the cereal box you read—designers create every detail. The last animated movie you watched? Someone created the cartoons while others wrote the story and the music!

In addition, advances in technology have affected every aspect of the art world. The invention of the **3-D printer** has been put to use by sculptors. Innovations in building materials make homes and structures safer and more environmentally friendly. Crafters share and sell their handmade products and services online, from jewelry to woodworking. Creativity rules in businesses of every type and size.

You will be amazed at the many ways science, engineering, math, and technology influence the entire world of art! Keep reading to explore creative ways to find your future in art. In each chapter, you'll find opportunities to...

## Surf the 'Net!

Type the words that are **bold** in the Surf the 'Net sections of this book into your favorite Internet search engine (like Google, Bing, or Yahoo) to find more information about each subject. Be sure to have permission and SUPERVISION from a trusted adult (like a teacher or parent) when using the Internet.

## Explore Some More!

In this book you'll find ideas you can use to explore cool resources in websites, in the news, and even in fun online games. Here's your chance to goof around and learn some more.

## Ask Big Questions!

Curiosity opens the door to learning (and fun!). Ponder the questions posed here. Each question comes with an activity you can do. Use them to share your answers with others through posters, games, presentations, or even a good discussion in which you consider both sides of an idea.

**Go online to download free activity sheets at www.cherrylakepublishing.com/activities.**

# Architect

## Surf the 'Net!

Take a trip around the world by searching online sites that let you virtually tour ancient architecture, such as the **Pyramids of Giza** in Egypt and **Machu Picchu** in Peru.

An **architect** is a person who plans and designs buildings. An architect designed the house you live in, the school you learn in, and the places you play in. First, they have to imagine these places. Then they have to create very detailed plans explaining how to build them.

Some architects design enormous buildings like the largest mall in your town or famous amusement parks like Disneyland. Others specialize in restoring historical buildings, like ancient castles in England and Ireland. Buildings of any size, shape, or purpose have first been imagined by architects.

Engineers continue to create new building materials that require fewer natural resources and to reuse existing materials. So if you are interested in helping the environment, now is a great time to explore a job in architecture.

The John Hancock Center in Chicago, Illinois, is a great feat of architecture. Tourists take a high-speed elevator up 1,000 feet (305 meters)—94 floors—to an observatory with glass walls and a glass floor. You can step on the clear floor, look down, and get a bird's-eye view of exactly how high you are. The person who designed that floor probably had fun imagining visitors' reactions—which range from totally amazed to totally freaked out!

Many architects are also engineers. Civil architects specialize in government buildings. They must follow strict safety rules about every aspect of the design. Rules make a difference. For instance, one innovation that helps keep people safe is the placement of

## Ask Big Questions!

Take a good look at your bedroom. **How can you use better design to make your living space safer and more comfortable?** Sketch out your ideas in a drawing or diagram.

## Explore Some More!

Learn more about architecture at this kid-friendly website: www. archKIDecture.org.

fluorescent signs. If the power goes out, these signs remain bright for as long as 48 hours. This helps people find their way around pitch-dark buildings. You might not think this is a big deal until the power goes out and you get stuck on the 20th floor of a skyscraper. These lights can literally save lives!

Architects are also artists, using their imaginations to express their art through their buildings. Tourists from around the world visit buildings designed by famous architect Frank Lloyd Wright. Many of his buildings are now considered historic landmarks and are open to the public for tours. Some can even be rented for the ultimate architectural vacation.

*America's most famous architect, Frank Lloyd Wright, designed this house and called it Fallingwater.*

# Cartoonist

**Surf the 'Net!**

Compare different styles of cartooning. **Anime** and **manga** are two styles of Japanese cartooning. Can you tell the difference?

Think of your favorite cartoon character. The last animated movie you saw. The characters in your video games.

**Cartoonists** bring cartoons to life in television, movies, video games, comic books, newspapers, and the Internet. Cartoons have evolved tremendously from the days of *Mickey Mouse*, one of the first and most famous animated cartoon characters. Cartoonists today have more than a great sense of humor.

Before computers, everything was drawn by hand. Animations were drawn picture by picture. When making the cartoon *Bambi*, the Disney studio became home to two live deer, Bambi and Felina, just like in the movie. The deer's muscles, behaviors, and movements inspired the artists' drawings to be more realistic.

Long after *Bambi*, Phil Vischer (Bob the Tomato) and Mike Nawrocki (Larry the Cucumber) came up with the idea of using funny vegetable cartoon characters to illuminate Bible stories. They tried to sell their story to **producers**. According to Nawrocki, none of the people they met with was willing to take a risk and back the project. But the two friends didn't give up.

They worked in Phil's garage to create the first *VeggieTales* movie. They brought their artistic idea to life, and the rest, as they say, is history. *VeggieTales* exploded into television episodes, full-length movies, and a massive line of entertainment products— toys, books, CDs, and video games. Phil and Mike's persistence paid off!

## Ask Big Questions!

Editorial cartoonists use humor in their art to send messages about important issues, like the environment or presidential election campaigns. **What current issue would you address if you were an editorial cartoonist?** Draw a sketch that makes a statement!

Advances in **animation software** and technology have completely changed the animation process from start to finish. Cartoonists (also called animators) still draw by hand today, but they use computers to give the cartoons movement and add special effects.

Advances in technology have also led to an entirely new industry for cartoonists—the **gaming industry**. Cartoonists can become game designers and create graphics for game developers. Some game designers create the look of the game, its levels, and the game's story line. Gaming has become so popular that hundreds of colleges now offer degrees in game development.

## Explore Some More!

Create stories, games, and animations to share with others at **scratch.mit.edu**. This free creative learning community is hosted by the Massachusetts Institute of Technology.

*Animators create the video game worlds that gamers like to visit.*

# Fashion Designer

## Surf the 'Net!

Find out how **recycled textiles** and **secondary materials** can be reused to make new products like carpet padding and furniture upholstery.

Did you ever look at your favorite shirt and wonder how the fabric was put together? Long ago, fabrics were woven by hand on a weaving loom. Thanks to technology, the cloth used for clothes, furniture, and curtains is now **mass-produced**, so you can easily find what you're looking for in your favorite stores.

Most clothing designers use math in many ways. The dress that costume designer Sandy Powell created for the main character in the 2015 film *Cinderella* was an artistic and mathematical invention. Powell started with a wire cage frame, then layered on dozens of delicate fabrics in different colors. The layers were topped with a fabric so thin it floated like smoke.

In order to sell more products, the fashion industry uses statistics to figure out what people want to wear. This information helps them decide things like what colors to use in clothing and what cartoon characters to put on T-shirts. Specialized fashion designers might create a new or limited style or expensive unique items.

Fashion industry professionals have to be forward-thinking and trendsetting. They have to know how fabrics are made and used. Textile designers create fabrics. They understand materials, dyes, patterns, and manufacturing processes. Others in the fashion industry work as stylists for magazine or catalog photo shoots. Some are store-window display designers who dress **mannequins** for high-end department stores.

## Ask Big Questions!

Fashion designers use geometry to create new designs by putting together patterns and angles in appealing ways. **Why do some fashion styles look better on certain body types than other types?** Make sketches of designs that work for someone of your size and shape.

## Explore Some More!

Become a fashion designer with KiZi's online video game Fashion Designer New York at **www.kizi.com/games/c/fashion-designer-new-york.**

*Fashion designers make sketches to illustrate their ideas.*

Costume designers are needed for theater productions and movies. They make clothing for films that take place in different eras. Costume designers visit museums to see clothing displays and then sketch the looks they want. For movies set in recent times, a costume designer might search in thrift stores for items that reflect the current styles.

Other designers use fashion to solve problems. Kevin Plank, the head of the athletic clothing company Under Armour™, found that certain fabrics worked better at soaking up sweat after a hard day of playing college football. Under Armour™ is now worn by athletes worldwide.

# Graphic Designer

## Surf the 'Net!

The copyright symbol was introduced in the U.S. in 1954. Search copyright to learn why it is very important for artists.

From the moment you wake up until it's time to close your eyes, the world of **graphic design** affects you. You might be exposed to thousands of images a day!

Everything that is not made by nature is designed by someone. A lot of thinking goes into the design of the things you read, play with, purchase, or consume. It's someone's job to decide what **font** to use, where to put the text, and what colors are best.

Graphic design works differently than other types of design because it involves your mental participation, even if you don't actually realize you are participating. Designs travel from your eyes to your mind, and when done right, design can get you to stop or start doing something. A perfect example is the red circle with a slash through it. You can probably picture it in your mind. It means "no!" and your brain gets this message very clearly.

On the pages of a magazine, **graphic designers** pay close attention to every detail that goes on every page—the text size, font, images, colors, and placement of every visual element. The cover and interior of books, the layout of your favorite website, the images in the online game you play, the logo of your hometown sports team, the signs on buildings—every detail was carefully chosen by a graphic designer.

A graphic designer typically works on a computer using design software such as Adobe InDesign or Adobe Illustrator.

## Ask Big Questions!

**How did magazines lay out artwork before the days of computers?** Before the digital age page layouts were done by hand. Use paper, scissors, glue, pictures, and text to create one or two pages of your own magazine.

Graphic designers need math skills to help with **page layout**, size, ratios, and scale. Sometimes a graphic designer will first sketch ideas on paper, then transfer the concepts to a digital format.

In the business world, graphic designers work for corporations, ad agencies, publishing companies, graphic design firms, and other businesses. But many graphic designers are **freelancers**, which means they work from their homes.

If you'd love to create children's books, design CD covers for bands, or design attention-grabbing billboards, you might make a terrific graphic designer!

## Explore Some More!

Take a look at a collaborative design project that is just for kids at kidsthinkdesign. org/products.

*Graphic designers use low-tech and high-tech tools to do their jobs.*

# Museum Curator

## Surf the 'Net!

Visit the world's most famous art museums online. What type of art do you like best?

Wouldn't it be cool to be a nighttime security guard in a museum where all the wax figures come to life after dark? *Night at the Museum* is a movie about a down-and-out dad who takes that job at the American Museum of Natural History in New York City. The movie is fictional, of course, and there's no magic that can bring museum artifacts to life. But even in this hilarious movie, viewers sense the awesomeness of the art collections as the **museum curator** leads Larry around on his first day.

The sequel, *Night at the Museum: Battle of the Smithsonian*, was partially filmed at the Smithsonian Institution. The Smithsonian Institution is the world's largest museum and research complex, located in Washington, D.C. It includes 19 museums and galleries, plus the National Zoo.

If you go there, you can see many famous artifacts. Able is the name of the monkey who flew into space in 1959. After he died, he was preserved and put on display at the National Air and Space Museum.

The boxing gloves of former heavyweight champion Muhammad Ali can be seen at the National Museum of American History. Both museums are part of the Smithsonian Institution. Smithsonian museums and the National Zoo are free and open every day except Christmas.

Museum curators get to decide what collections to exhibit in their museums. They see all kinds of amazing artifacts and

## Ask Big Questions!

If you were a museum curator what kind of exhibit would you like to create? Use a shoebox to create a diorama or make sketches of your ideas.

## Explore Some More!

Imagine what it would be like to live in a museum. Begin your adventure taking a virtual tour of the Smithsonian Institution and its massive and amazing cluster of museums at www.si.edu/Kids.

works of art when making their decisions. Curators know much about art history, and some specialize further, such as in **archaeology** for natural history museums.

Nearly every city and town has its own museums, and curators seek out all kinds of displays. The planet's largest collection of roller skates is at the National Museum of Roller Skating in Nebraska. The Vent Haven Ventriloquist Museum in Kentucky is home to 750 dummies. You can ham it up at the SPAM museum in Minnesota, or go bananas at the International Banana Museum in California.

When it comes to museums, there is truly something for everyone!

*The world's great works of arts, like Michelangelo's Statue of David, are housed in museums.*

# Product Designer

From your skateboard, to a three-ring binder, to the magic toilet that flushes itself in public restrooms, **product designers** envision and engineer almost every object or device you use in everyday life.

Product designers work with all kinds of people and industries. Almost every single thing you can think of—cars, toys, houses, TVs, computers, and smartphones—has been invented, created, patented, and produced in some way.

## Surf the 'Net!

Kids and teens have invented everything from health treatments to handy gadgets. Search **young inventors** to see some of the brilliant innovations created by kids like you.

For painters who work on a canvas, a product designer came up with the easel, the style of paintbrush, and the texture of the canvas. Some product designers specialize in environmentally friendly buildings. Some create alternative power sources to conserve natural resources, like windmills.

Product designers brainstorm ideas, often in teams, for new products or for ways to update existing products, like the next best sports car or technological gadget. Creative thinking is how great new products are born.

Many product designers today use 3-D printers to **conceptualize** and create a **prototype**. Once the product's design is fine-tuned, it goes on to be manufactured and **mass-marketed**. Designers also engineer how products are manufactured. They then follow through to make sure everything works once completed.

Some inventive product designers not only design products, but also rethink

## Ask Big Questions!

People come up with product designs because they have a vision. **What new product do you think the world needs?** Break out your childhood building blocks, an erector set, some molding clay, or any other material of your choice and create a rough prototype of your product idea.

how their products are made. Take Aly Khalifa, founder of LYF Shoes. Aly designed shoes that can be made of completely recyclable materials. Customers pick the style they want and Aly uses a special process to measure each customer's foot size. Then he uses 3-D printers to produce the coolest, most comfortable shoes his customers have ever worn! When the shoes wear out, customers disassemble all the parts and put them in recycle bins.

Good design makes products we use every day more useful, attractive, and enjoyable. And you never know where you'll find inspiration for the next big product!

## Explore Some More!

Learn to think like a designer at **www. kidsthinkdesign.org**. It offers programs in not only product design but also fashion design, graphic design, interior design, book design, architecture, animation, and more.

*3-D printers are changing the way products are imagined and produced.*

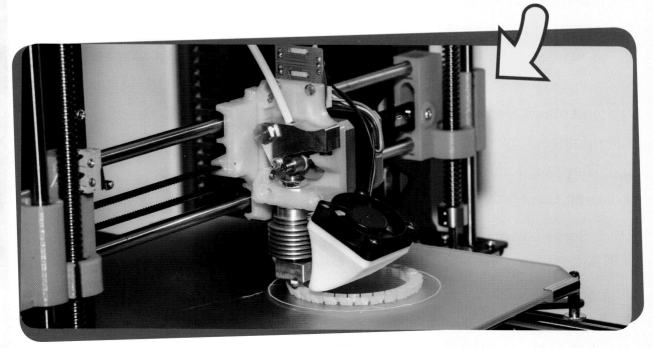

# Set Designer

## Surf the 'Net!

Search for **community theater** and find out what makes up the set design at a production of a play.

Almost all television shows, movies, and theater productions need a **set designer**. This is the person who decorates the stage to set the environment for whatever is being played out onstage or in a studio.

Many films are shot on location in places like blocked-off city streets for a car chase or inside a real hospital for a medical scene. But even those sets need to be "dressed up" to fit the details of the production.

The movie *Camp Rock* was filmed in Ontario, Canada, at two real camp resorts, using existing cabins, recreation halls, and other structures. But set decorators still went to work hanging banners and furnishing cabins and rec areas with props to make the atmosphere fit the tone of the movie.

Many television shows are filmed on a **soundstage**, while live plays are performed on a theater stage. In both cases, a production that is set in a school, for example, would require the set designer to build a school setting, rather than film inside an actual school. Lockers, desks, chairs, shelves, walls with doors to separate classrooms, and other props make the stage look like a real school.

Those desks and shelves would need to be filled with books, binders, and school supplies. Walls might be painted to look like the brick wall of a school and then painted again with graffiti for an authentic rough neighborhood feel.

## Ask Big Questions!

**If producers were making a movie about the story of your life, what would the set design look like?** Sketch out ideas or take photos of your favorite hangouts and make a collage.

## Explore Some More!

Get your ideas flowing with team challenges that teach concepts behind design thinking. Everything you need to participate can be found at Cooper Hewitt's "Ready, Set, Design" site, **www.cooperhewitt. org/2011/09/09/ready-set-design**.

A construction crew works onstage or on location to build the parts of the set that require carpentry work, like the stage in *Camp Rock* where the Jonas Brothers performed.

Thanks to modern technology some movie sets exist only on computers. This is true for movies based in outer space like *Star Wars*. In some scenes, actors perform in front of blank green screens and designers add visuals by way of amazing animation technology.

Many set designers live in areas where a lot of films or plays are produced, such as New York or Hollywood. They all get to travel a lot and meet celebrities and actors.

*This set was home to Bilbo Baggins in* The Hobbit *movie.*

# Writer

Now is an exciting time for anyone who wants to be a **writer**, especially kids. Age doesn't matter in the writing industry, and you're never too young to start. Publishers are companies that print your writings, and more than ever, publishers and **media** experts want to hear from you. Many seek out young writers, and books have been written by kids at young ages.

Christopher Paolini started his award-winning *Eragon* when he was 15. Juliette

Turner was 11 when she started writing her first book, *Our Constitution Rocks!*

Writers write for many **genres**. There are novelists, sports reporters, investigative journalists, poets, songwriters, magazine columnists, scriptwriters, ad copywriters, textbook authors, and Web content providers. New opportunities continue to arise with advances in computers.

A writer can write about any topic, and the subject matter is truly limitless. Someone who is interested in medicine and loves to write might contribute to medical books and health-related websites. Many websites and online magazines have editorial staffs just like print magazines, and websites offer hundreds of places for writers to submit their work. You can even submit your homework papers as articles to online and print magazines!

Of course, not all writers are *writers*. Their real job may be lawyer or public relations director or scientist or any other job where communicating ideas and information is part of a day's work. Some people are

## Ask Big Questions!

**What do you like to write about?** Writing is a skill everyone puts to good use now and then, whether jotting a note in a birthday card or drafting a fan letter to your sports idol. Imagine that you are a writer and write a story about what your job is like.

surprised at how much writing is involved in so many different types of jobs.

All writers are also readers. Books, articles, newspapers, and other media help writers see different writing styles. Getting familiar with what kinds of writing are out there is an important tool in improving writing skills.

Writing takes dedication. You have to make time, set goals, and get feedback from others, like your English teacher or a writers' group. Writing talent comes very naturally when you let go and let the creativity flow! But writing is also a craft that continues to improve over time. It's never too early to start honing your craft as a writer!

## Explore Some More!

*Teen Ink* is a magazine, website, and series of books written by teens. Go to www.TeenInk.com to subscribe, submit your work, or join a teen writers' workshop.

*Writers and books go together like shoes and socks!*

# Find *Your* Future in Art

Let's review the amazing career ideas you've just discovered. Below are descriptions of some of the opportunities waiting for people who like art. Read them and see if you can match them with the correct job titles.

*Please do not write in this book. Use a separate sheet of paper to write your answers and imagine your future! Or, better yet, go online to download a free activity sheet at www.cherrylakepublishing.com/activities.*

**A** Architect

**B** Cartoonist

**C** Fashion designer

**D** Graphic designer

**E** Museum curator

**F** Product designer

**G** Set designer

**H** Writer

**1** Decides what to put on a cereal box

**2** Uses words to tell stories in commercials

**3** Uses computer software to animate illustrations

**4** Helps keep people safe inside buildings

**5** Designs a car that runs on garbage

**6** Creates costumes for movies

**7** Works with lots of ancient artifacts and treasures

**8** Decides what buildings and props are needed for a theatrical performance

(Answer Key: 1-D; 2-H; 3-B; 4-A; 5-F; 6-C; 7-E; 8-G

# Glossary

**3-D printer** process that uses computers and special printing devices to build new, three-dimensional products from layers of materials such as plastic or metal

**animation software** computer programs used by cartoonists or illustrators for generating animated images

**archaeology** the science of studying the bones, tools, and artifacts of ancient people

**architect** person who designs buildings and supervises the way they are constructed

**artifacts** objects created by humans that remain from a particular period in the past

**cartoonist** visual artist who specializes in drawing cartoons for entertainment, political commentary, or advertising

**conceptualize** to invent or formulate an idea or concept

**fashion designer** person who uses an understanding of fabrics to create clothes

**freelancer** person who works for different clients instead of one employer

**font** set of type (letters and numbers) that share an overall design, including size, weight (thickness), and style

**gaming industry** the economic sector involved with the development, marketing, and sales of video games

**genres** particular kinds of creative work, such as science fiction and fantasy

**graphic design** process of visual communication

**graphic designers** artists who use combinations of type (letters and numbers), visual arts, and page layout techniques to create and produce a final result

**mannequin** a dummy used to display clothes in a store window

**mass-marketed** advertising or promotion of a product, good, or service to as many people as possible

**mass-produced** made by making many copies of products very quickly, using assembly line techniques

**media** the main means of communication with large numbers of people (especially through television, radio, newspapers, and the Internet)

**museum curator** person who manages collections of artifacts or works of art in a museum

**page layout** the part of graphic design that deals with the arrangement of visual elements on a page

**producer** person in charge of making and usually finding the money for a play, movie, recording, or media

**prototype** the first version of an invention that tests an idea to see if it will work

**product designer** person who creates a new product for a business to sell to its customers

**set designer** person who creates the setting for theatrical, film, or television scenery

**soundstage** large, soundproof studio used for filming motion pictures or television shows

**writer** person who writes books, stories, or articles

# Index

## About the Author

Kim Childress is an award-winning editor and author of more than 300 books, short stories, and articles for kids and the parents in their lives. She gets lots of writing inspiration from her personal focus group of four children, ages 12 to 20. Kim has also worked as a reviewer, newspaper reporter, newspaper advertising sales executive, bookseller, landscaper, real estate title writer, theater check-in girl, waitress, hostess, and professional ice-cream scooper. Learn more at her website, www.ChildressInk.com.